This Book Belongs To:

Today I Am Feeling:

MULTIRAY. Copyright 2025. All Rights Reserved.

Feelings are everywhere, and your body knows their secret language. When you listen, you learn how to guide them—and that makes you the hero of your own mind, heart, and body.

HOW MY FEELINGS TALK

By H. J. Ray

Have you ever felt angry?
I have.

Anger makes my heart race and my head feel hot.

But if I take a sloooooow breath — in... and out...
I can soothe my angry feeling, and think about something that helps me feel better.

Like love.
Have you ever felt loving?
I have.

Love makes my heart feel like it's glowing and my body feels lighter and brighter.

When I feel loving,
I want to do kind things for others.

To me,
love is time with my favourite people, and
a warm hug.

Have you ever felt scared?
I have.

Scared makes my knees feel wobbly,
and my heart race so fast
it feels like it might leap out of my mouth!

Sometimes I feel scared
before I jump into the ocean,
or when I walk into a room full of people I don't know.
But deep down...
I want to dive in —
to splash, to smile,
to make new friends.
That's when I try to focus on a different feeling...
I try to feel...

Brave.
Have you ever felt brave?
I have.

Brave makes me feel taller,
and stronger from the inside.

When I feel brave, sometimes I can still hear
my scared thoughts, but they are more quiet.

When i'm brave, I feel proud of myself.

Because I can choose
which feeling to focus on.

Have you ever felt upset?

Sometimes, when I feel upset,
I go very quiet.
My chest feels tight,
and I stare at my feet.

Other times,
I'm so upset that I cry—a lot.

Sometimes, I ask for a hug.
Sometimes, I talk about what's bothering me.
Other times, drawing helps me feel better.

And slowly,
I find my way back to feeling...

**Happy.
Oh yes, I love feeling happy!**

When I feel happy,
I feel light and free.

Happy is one of my favourite feelings.
And I've learned something that helps me stay happy:
The food I eat,
how much sleep I get,
can really change my mood.

Because if I don't sleep well,
or I eat too much junk food,
my body just feels...

Tired.
Have you ever felt tired?

When I'm tired,
it's hard to feel happy.

I feel lazy,
and a bit grumpy.

But if I tell people how I'm feeling,
it helps them understand.

Then I have a rest,
or something cheers me up—
and I'm back to my usual, energised, sometimes...

Silly self.
Yep, I really love feeling silly!

It's hard to explain silly,
but it's like...
jumping jelly beans in my pants!

I don't feel like sitting still—
I feel like wiggling and jiggling,
climbing and giggling,
being loud and playful with my friends.

Until my little brother walks into the room,
all silly too—
and breaks something.

Then I feel...

Annoyed.
Have you ever felt annoyed?

Annoyed feels a bit like angry—
but smaller.

I don't really like feeling annoyed,
because sometimes,
one small annoying thing
makes everything else feel annoying too.

Annoyed feels like a bad taste in my mouth
that I just can't get rid of.

But I've learned a little trick
that helps me feel really...

Calm.
Have you ever felt calm?

To me, calm feels like soft butter.
It's a mix of love and happiness,
all melted together.

If calm had a taste,
it would be fresh-baked cookies with milk.

When I feel calm,
I just know it's going to be a great day.

But just like milk and cookies,
calm doesn't last forever—
and that's okay.

Even if I feel...

Confused.
Have you ever felt confused?

Confused feels like
a lot of thoughts in my head —
all talking at once.

But if I stop focusing on what's confusing,
get out of my head and into my body...
and I play a sport,
draw a picture,
or spend time with a friend,
my thoughts start to untangle.

Because feelings don't
last forever.

And I like to practice the ones
that feel good.
And here's the best part...
I always make better choices
from a feeling like...

Excitement.
Ohhh, I really love feeling excited!

Excited feels like brave,
and happy,
and loving,
and calm—
with a little bit of silliness sprinkled in!

It's like tiny bubbles in my tummy—
like soda fizz
and butterfly wings
flapping all at once.

Or the feeling of seeing
the most amazing cake ever...
and knowing it's all yours.

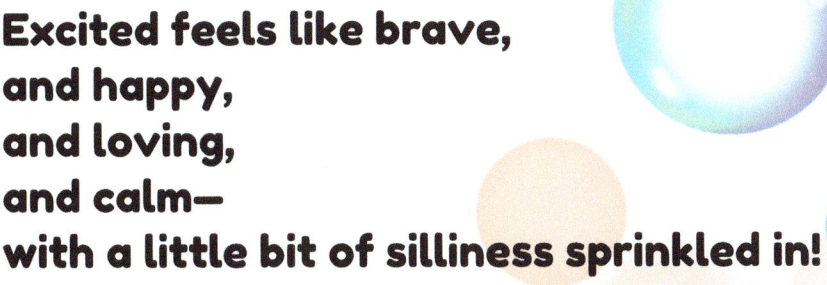

Did you enjoy exploring feelings with me?

I'd love to hear what you thought! Leaving a review helps more kids and families join the feelings adventure.

www.multiray.com.au

Hi, I'm Heather Ray—an author, illustrator, and wellbeing educator. I create resources that help children (and their grown-ups!) explore feelings, nurture resilience, and care for their mental health.

I believe the art of feeling good is a skill we can all learn. When we start young, keep the conversation flowing, and hold space for emotions, we raise children who are happy, compassionate, confident, and self-aware.

Through my books, workshops, and wellbeing programs, I love showing families and educators that emotions aren't problems to be fixed—they're messages to be understood. With mindfulness, creativity, and play, we can make even the biggest feelings easier to talk about and navigate together.

www.multiray.com.au

✨ More books on feelings and emotions by H. J. Ray ✨

✨ Your Next Step: Get Support & Resources ✨

✨ Visit www.multiray.com.au ✨

www.ingramcontent.com/pod-product-compliance
Lightning Source LLC
Chambersburg PA
CBHW041203290426
44109CB00003B/114